Les Paul

GUITAR WIZARD

BOB JACOBSON

Wisconsin Historical Society Press

Published by the Wisconsin Historical Society Press
Publishers since 1855

© 2012 by State Historical Society of Wisconsin

wisconsin**history**.org

Photographs identified with WHi are from the Society's collections; address requests to reproduce these photos to the Visual Materials Archivist at Wisconsin Historical Society, 816 State Street, Madison, WI 53706.

Unless otherwise noted, all other images are property of the Les Paul Foundation. Please direct inquiries about such photos to the Les Paul Foundation, 236 West 30th Street 7th Floor, New York, NY 10001.

Printed in Wisconsin, U.S.A.
Designed by Jill Bremigan

16 15 14 13 12   1 2 3 4 5

Library of Congress Cataloging-in-Publication Data

Jacobson, Bob.
  Les Paul : guitar wizard / Bob Jacobson.
     p. cm. — (Badger biographies)
  Includes bibliographical references and index.
  ISBN 978-0-87020-488-3 (pbk. : alk. paper) 1. Paul, Les—Juvenile literature. 2. Guitarists—United States—Biography—Juvenile literature. I. Title.
  ML3930.P29J33 2012
  787.87092—dc23
  [B]
                          2011033617

Front and back cover: Courtesy of the Les Paul Foundation

∞The paper used in this publication meets the minimum requirements of the American National Standard for Information Sciences—Permanence of Paper for Printed Library Materials, ANSI Z39.48-1992.

Les Paul

Other Badger Biographies

This book is dedicated to every person who ever twiddled a knob, plucked or bowed a string, buzzed a mouthpiece, vibrated a reed, or bent an electronic circuit in hopes of sharing with the rest of the world a perfect sound they could hear inside their head. One of those people is my father. He gets a slightly bigger share of the dedication than everybody else for making sure we always had plenty of musical toys around the house, launching me on my own modest sound-chasing journey from an early age.

This book was made possible, in part, by a generous donation of photographs from the Les Paul Foundation. Additional funding was provided by a grant from the John C. Geillfuss fellowship fund.

Contents

1

Who Was Les Paul?

Imagine you are a 15-year-old boy from **Waukesha**, Wisconsin. Imagine you have already learned how to play the guitar and **harmonica** as well as most of the famous musicians you hear on the radio. You have already taught yourself how to take apart a radio, a record player, and a **player piano**—and put them back together. Now imagine you have the chance to go **on tour** as a **professional** musician 400 miles away. You ask your mother if it's okay. And she says, "It's your life. It's up to you!"

You are imagining the early life of Les Paul. From the time he was very young, Les was very good at figuring out how to make things work in new and better ways. He invented machines that have changed the way people make music. He came up with big plans for his musical career, and somehow

---

Waukesha: waw kuh shaw   **harmonica**: a small musical instrument that you play by blowing out and breathing in through the mouthpiece   **player piano**: a piano that can play by itself by reading holes punched in a roll of paper   **on tour**: traveling to different places to perform   **professional**: making money doing something that others do for fun

1

he made them happen. And as he got older and struggled with physical problems, he discovered a whole new way to play the guitar so he could continue to share his music with audiences.

Have you ever heard somebody play a guitar very loudly? Of course you have. Until Les Paul started inventing, that was impossible to do. Before Les built the world's first electric guitar, most guitars were **acoustic**. It was very difficult for acoustic guitars to be heard over the other instruments in a band.

Have you ever heard a song on the radio in which all the **harmony** parts were sung by the same person? Of course you have. That's done using a method called **multitrack recording**. In multitrack recording, one voice or "track" is recorded, then another track is recorded on top of it, then another, and so on until many voices and instruments can be heard in the same song. Les Paul was the person who invented a way of recording this "layered" effect. But these were not his only inventions. Les was also responsible for a long list of **technological breakthroughs** related to sound.

acoustic (uh **koo** stik): doesn't use electricity to change the sound or make it louder   **harmony**: the sounding of 2 or more musical notes that go well together   **multitrack recording**: a recording method in which many different parts are recorded at different times into one song   **technological breakthrough**: a discovery that solves a problem in the fields of science and engineering

2

And Les wasn't just an inventor. He was also one of the greatest guitar players of his time. During the 1950s, he and his wife and musical partner Mary Ford recorded several songs that became huge **hits**. Many of these songs are still well-known today.

Les was able to **accomplish** these things because he believed in himself. One of the reasons he believed in himself was because his mother believed in him, too. She always encouraged him to try things out and follow his dreams. So, when he took her radio apart, she didn't yell at him. And when he left home at 17 to be a professional musician, she rode on the bus with him to his new home in Saint Louis, Missouri. Not every kid with a **supportive** mother grows up to become a living **legend**. But it doesn't hurt.

Les with his Gibson L-5, one of his favorite guitars

hit: something that becomes popular or successful   **accomplish**: do or complete something successfully
supportive: helping or encouraging someone   **legend**: someone who is famous or well-known for something they've done

2

Whiz Kid from Waukesha

Les Paul wasn't always Les Paul. When he was born on June 9, 1915 in Waukesha, his parents named him Lester William **Polsfuss**. It is not surprising that Lester loved music even as a small child. His mother, **Evelyn**, was a very good piano player. When Les was young, his mother would play old German songs she had learned as a child.

Les's father, George, ran an auto repair business called George's Garage. George gave Les the nickname "Red" because of his red hair, and friends and family called him Red for much of his life. While Les had a very close relationship with his mother, he wasn't close with his father. George preferred to spend his time drinking alcohol and **gambling** with his friends. Sometimes George won unusual things gambling. Once he even won a hotel in downtown Waukesha. But he usually ended up losing these same things later.

Polsfuss: **pawl** fuhs   **Evelyn**: ev uh luhn   **gambling**: betting money on the outcome of a race, game, or contest

Les's parents **separated** when he was very young. Evelyn had to raise Les and his older brother Ralph on her own. George continued to live in Waukesha, but he was no longer part of Les's daily life. Many years later, when Les was famous and his father had given up his wild lifestyle, the 2 of them became closer.

At first, Evelyn thought Ralph would be the musician of the family. She bought Ralph a saxophone. But Ralph was not interested in music and did not seem to

The Polsfuss home
320 West St. Paul Avenue

Les Paul's childhood home

separated: stopped living together as husband and wife

5

Ralph and Les as kids

have natural talent. Les, on the other hand, couldn't get enough of music. He always wanted to listen to the radio or **crank up** the **phonograph**. His mother had a player piano, and Les loved to work the pump and watch the keys go up and down as it played. By listening and watching the keys, he learned which keys made the different notes sound.

Les never did **rely** on reading music. Legend has it that he never even learned how. He learned everything by ear, even after he grew up and became a professional musician. Soon Evelyn signed Les up to learn how to play the piano from a teacher who gave lessons just outside Waukesha.

Les and Ralph were different in another way as well. Ralph did not care so much about how things worked. But Les was

crank up: make something run by turning a crank   **phonograph** (**foh** nuh graf): an old-fashioned record player that used a crank instead of being plugged in   **rely**: depend on

6

very curious about electricity and machines. He always wanted to know what made a bulb light up, or what made a motor turn. Even after he had learned how something worked, he always wanted to figure out how to make it work *better*.

Les was lucky that his mother **approved** of his curiosity. His curious nature often got him into

Les's mother, Evelyn Polsfuss

trouble. But instead of scolding him, his mother was proud of his creativity—as long as he didn't do too much damage! And this curiosity prepared Les for the 2 **passions** that would stay with him for the rest of his life: music and **electronics**.

Les with his mother. Evelyn supported Les in his experiments and his desire to become a musician.

approved: had a good opinion   **passion (pash** uhn): great interest   **electronics**: appliances and equipment, such as microwave ovens, computers, televisions, and radar, that work by means of electricity

7

3

A Budding Musician and Inventor

Les got his first musical instrument when he was about 10 years old. One day, some workmen were digging up the street near the Polsfuss's house. During their lunch break, one of the workers pulled out a harmonica and started to play. As soon as he heard the sound, Les was fascinated.

The worker saw how interested Les was in the harmonica, and asked Les if he wanted to try it out. Les was so excited about the harmonica that the workman told him he could keep it. But just playing it was not enough for Les. He also had to know how it worked. He took the metal sides off to see what it was that made the sound. Fortunately, he was also clever enough to put the harmonica back together.

Les began playing the harmonica every possible moment. He could **imitate** the songs he heard on the radio. His constant harmonica playing drove his mother crazy. But she was patient with him and encouraged his new musical adventure.

Around the same time, Les began to experiment with electronics. He became interested in radios when a friend showed him the crystal radio he was building. A crystal radio is a very simple kind of radio that does not need a battery or a plug. It gets electrical power through an **antenna**. Some people still make their own crystal radios today because they

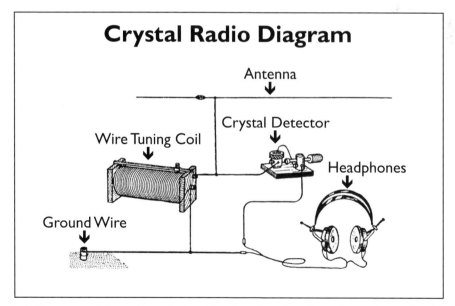

Crystal Radio Diagram

Antenna

Crystal Detector

Wire Tuning Coil

Headphones

Ground Wire

imitate: copy or mimic   **antenna** (an **ten** uh): a piece of metal or wire used to send or receive radio signals

are simple. They can be put together using ordinary materials like copper wire and a crystal "detector," which can pick up radio signals from the air. The crystal radio was very exciting to Les because radio had only been around for a few years. The idea that he could make a **device** that would allow him to listen to music from far away was amazing.

As it happened, a radio station based in Milwaukee had its **transmitter** in the countryside just outside of Waukesha. It was located close to where Les rode his bicycle every week for his piano lesson. Les began to visit the radio station on the days he had lessons. That's how he became friends with the **engineer** who kept the transmitter running. The engineer liked Les and was happy to teach him how radio **broadcasting** worked.

This was a wonderful time for Les. He was quickly getting good at playing the harmonica. He was learning how radios worked from the engineer at the radio station. And best of all, his mother let him use their living room as his own **laboratory**! The living room had a lot of things in it for Les

device: a piece of equipment that does a particular job **transmitter**: a device for sending out radio waves **engineer**: someone who is specially trained to build and maintain machines **broadcasting**: sending out a radio or television program to an audience **laboratory** (**lab** ruh tor ree): a room that has special equipment for people to use in scientific experiments

to experiment on: his mother's player piano, a big crank phonograph, a radio, and a telephone. Les loved to take these machines apart and put them back together. In fact, it wasn't long before he knew how the player piano worked better than the salesman his mother bought it from!

Player pianos work by reading patterns of holes punched into rolls of paper. Les began making his own sounds by punching holes in the blank ends of the paper rolls. If he didn't like the sound they made, he would put tape over the holes and punch new ones in different spots on the paper. Through

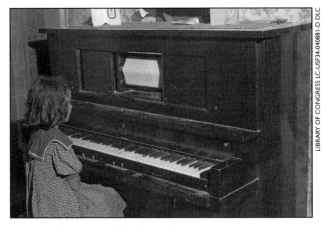

Les was fascinated by the player piano.

trial and error, he soon learned how to create music for the player piano!

trial and error: the process of trying or testing something and learning from mistakes

When Les had a question about how something worked, his mother helped him track down the answer. For example, he was curious about why the music on a phonograph record would play in a lower **pitch** when he slowed it down with his finger, but the notes on the player piano did not change when he slowed it down. Evelyn took him to the middle school to talk to the science teacher.

Les loved to experiment on his family's phonograph.

It turned out that the player piano was an early form of digital recording, like the kind people do on computers today. In digital recording, the sounds are recorded as a **series** of numbers. The numbers are then read by a machine, which turns the numbers back into sounds. A player piano uses the holes in the paper like a digital recorder uses numbers.

pitch: the highness or lowness of a musical sound **series**: a set of items that come one after another

Phonograph records, on the other hand, are **analog** recordings. The sound on a record is made up of tiny grooves that run in a spiral track around the center of the record. These grooves are made directly from the sounds of the instruments. They do not have to be changed into numbers— or holes in paper—to be played again. The sounds get lower when the record spins slowly, and higher when the record spins quickly.

Though he was fascinated by these early recording inventions, the thing Les loved best was the music. All of his curiosity about machines came from his desire to find better ways of making music and listening to music. Les listened to the radio as much as he could. Using the crystal radio he made himself and a spring on his bed for an antenna, Les often stayed up very late at night listening to whatever radio stations he could pick up. Some of them were as far away as Saint Louis, Missouri, and Nashville, Tennessee—hundreds of miles away!

analog (**an** uh log): showing information with moving parts, instead of numbers

Radio Station Call Letters

The letters that make up the name of a radio station, like WLS and WBBM in Chicago, are called "call letters" or "call signs." This way of naming radio stations was borrowed from an earlier form of communicating by radio. Beginning in the early 1900s, ships used radio waves to send **telegraph** messages to each other. In 1912, representatives from several countries came up with a system to identify ships. Each ship would have a 3-letter code that was different from every other ship's code, and each country's ships would have codes starting with a certain letter. The United States decided that ships on the East Coast would have letter codes beginning with K, and ships on the West Coast would have codes beginning with W.

The system was soon used on land as well. By the time radio stations starting springing up all over the country in the 1920s, call signs had grown to 4 letters. And for some reason that nobody can really explain, the W and K got switched around. Radio stations east of the Mississippi River started with W, and stations west of the Mississippi started with K. That system remains in place to this day.

telegraph: a device for sending messages long distances by wire or radio using a code of electrical signals

One of Les's favorite **radio musicians** was a man known as Pie Plant Pete. Pete had his own radio show on WLS, a station in Chicago, Illinois, where he played old-time country music that was sometimes called **hillbilly**. He sang funny songs and **accompanied** himself on guitar and harmonica. When Pie Plant Pete came to play in Waukesha, Les's mother took him to see the show. Les got one of the biggest thrills of his young life when he got to meet Pete backstage after the show. Pete even let Les hold his guitar!

Les got his first guitar in 1927, when he was 11 years old. The guitar was an inexpensive **model** from the Sears & Roebuck **catalog**. It cost less than 5 dollars. Les quickly taught himself how to

Les's mom made him a sailor suit like Pie Plant Pete's.

radio musician: someone who performs music live on the radio   **hillbilly**: a type of country music from the South, often played on fiddles, banjos, and guitars   **accompanied**: played along on a musical instrument   **model**: a particular type or design of a product   **catalog**: a magazine listing things you can buy from a company

play some **chords**. His goal, of course, was to sound just like Pie Plant Pete. To do that, he had to figure out how to play harmonica and guitar at the same time. He did it by making a special harmonica holder out of coat hanger wire—his first invention! The special holder allowed him to flip the harmonica over with his chin. That way, he could play it on whichever side had the right notes for the song he was playing.

Les picked his first guitar out of a catalog like this one from Sears & Roebuck.

chord (kord): 2 or more musical notes played at the same time

4

Les Takes the Stage

As Les practiced the guitar and harmonica, he got better and better. Before long he started looking for audiences. He would play for anybody willing to listen. Pretty soon, he was able to draw a crowd whenever he started playing. His mother gave him the nickname "Red Hot Red," and that was the name people all over Waukesha came to know him by. Les was a **natural** performer. He never got nervous playing in front of an audience. It seemed as if that was exactly what he was born to do.

Red Hot Red put together a band, and they began to play around town at dances, restaurants, and even beach parties on Lake Michigan. They would play for **tips** wherever they were allowed. The rest of the time, they played for free. When Les was 13, he gave his first paid performance. For the first time, he was paid an amount agreed upon before the show.

natural: a person who has a special talent or ability   **tips**: money given to someone as thanks for service

Downtown Waukesha in the 1930s

That show, at the **Schroeder** Hotel in Milwaukee, officially made him a professional **entertainer**!

Les continued to play all over Waukesha. One of his regular stops in town was a popular **drive-in** restaurant called Beekman's **Barbecue** Stand. Les could usually count on taking in a lot of tips when he played at Beekman's. Cars full of customers filled the parking lot. But Les thought he could make even more money if he could make his sound **carry** a greater distance. That way, the people in the cars parked farther away would be able to hear him.

So he became an inventor again. Les **devised** his own microphone using the mouthpiece from a telephone and the speaker from his mother's radio. And it worked!

Schroeder: **shray** dur   **entertainer**: someone who performs in public   **drive-in**: a restaurant where customers are served food in their cars   **barbecue**: **bahr** buh kyoo   **carry**: travel over a distance
devised: thought of a new way to do or create something

18

Red Hot Red loved to perform with his band. Les is in the middle with his harmonica and guitar.

The next time Les performed at the barbeque stand, he got a note from someone in the back. It said, "Red, your voice and harmonica are fine, but your guitar's not loud enough." Les the Inventor to the rescue again! This time, Les took the needle and **tone arm** from his family's phonograph and attached them to the **bridge** of his guitar. When he played the guitar, the sound came through the phonograph speaker. The **sound quality** was not very good, but Les had just made his first electric guitar! His ability to sing and play louder

tone arm: the arm of a phonograph that holds the needle that reads the record   **bridge**: the thin piece of wood or plastic that holds a guitar's strings above the body of the instrument   **sound quality**: the degree of excellence of the sound

meant he made a lot more in tips ... except on days when his mother wanted to use the phonograph.

Les continued to experiment with his electric guitar to improve the sound. He tested many materials that would **conduct** electricity, including a steel railroad rail and a railroad spike. Meanwhile, Les was still experimenting

Les experimented with building an electric guitar by using a piece of a railroad track to conduct electricity.

with radios. Before long, he had set up his own miniature broadcasting station right in his home.

His next project was to learn how to record the music he was playing. For help, Les turned to the head **mechanic** at his father's garage. The mechanic gave him a **flywheel** from an old car motor. To turn the flywheel, Les asked his dentist for the kind of **belt** used on dental drills at the time. With help from the mechanic, Les built a recording machine that worked by

conduct: allow something to pass through   **mechanic** (muh **kan** ik): a person who repairs machines
flywheel: a heavy wheel that turns at a steady speed to make a machine run smoothly   **belt**: a circular band of rubber used to transfer motion from one part of a machine to another

cutting grooves with a nail into an **aluminum disk**—similar to recording a song on a record.

Les got help with his inventions from a mechanic at his father George Polsfuss's garage.

While he was building these machines, Les continued to get better as a musician. Mostly, he imitated the songs he heard Pie Plant Pete and other popular performers play on the radio. And soon, Les was good enough to play on the radio himself! The first station he played on was WRJN, a small station in **Racine**, a town outside of Milwaukee. Soon he was playing on bigger stations in Milwaukee. He also starting playing **live** shows at big theaters, like the Uptown Theater in Milwaukee, where he still **appeared** under the name Red Hot Red.

aluminum: uh **loo** muh nuhm   disk: a flat, circular object   **Racine**: ruh **seen**   **live** (lɪv): broadcast while actually being performed, not recorded before   **appeared**: performed on television, radio, or live

One day a band called **Rube Tronson** and His Texas Cowboys came to perform a concert in a nearby town. Les had heard this band on the radio and liked them. So he and some of his friends went to the show. At the show, Les was amazed by the band's guitar player, a young man named Sunny Joe **Wolverton**. Sunny Joe noticed how much attention Les was paying him.

When the band took a break, he started talking to Les. Sunny Joe asked him if he played the guitar. Les told Joe he did play some guitar, and Joe showed him some fancy guitar tricks. Joe told Les to practice what he showed him and come back in 2 weeks, when the band was playing in another town not far from Waukesha. Les came back 2 weeks later to show Joe what he had learned. Joe was impressed.

Over the next several weeks, Joe gave Les more guitar **tips**. Soon Les had gotten so good that Joe and the bandleader, Rube Tronson, decided to let him come onstage and play a song with them. Les played so well that at the end of the night Rube offered him a job with the band.

Rube Tronson: roob **tron** suhn   **Wolverton**: **wohl** vur tuhn   **tip**: a helpful piece of advice

At first, Les was sure that there was no way he would be able to join the band. After all, he was still in school. But as usual, his mother was very supportive of his musical activities. She told Les that it was okay as long as he agreed to play with the band during summer vacation. He would return to school when summer was over. It helped that Les was going to be

Les toured with Rube Tronson's band the summer he was 15. Sunny Joe is on the far left, and Rube is second from the right.

23

paid $10 a night, which was quite a lot of money in those days!

But there was also an unpleasant surprise: Sunny Joe, who had taught Les so much, had been fired from the band. Les was being hired to take his place! Still, Les spent the summer **touring** with the Texas Cowboys. He got his first chance to see the wild and sometimes rough life of the traveling musician up close. Musicians who constantly travel from town to town meet lots of different kinds of people. And because they usually work at night, they sometimes don't get enough sleep.

But many traveling musicians have great adventures! Even so, Les was not yet ready to have that kind of life *all* the time. After all, he was only 15. As he had promised his mother, at the end of the summer Les quit the Texas Cowboys. He moved back home and went back to school.

One day in the early fall of 1932, Les got an unexpected phone call. It was Sunny Joe Wolverton. Les had not spoken with Joe for over a year. Joe was working as a musician for a radio station in Saint Louis, Missouri. He invited Les to come

touring: traveling to different places to perform

24

and join him there as part of a country music band he was **forming** for a radio program. Of course Les wanted to go, but he was still in school.

Once again, Les talked to his mother. And once again, his mother was supportive. She knew that if Les went off to join Joe in Saint Louis, it meant he was probably quitting high school for good, without **graduating**. But she also knew that he had a gift for music and that playing music made him happier than anything else. So together, she and Les took a Greyhound bus to Saint Louis. When they arrived, she told Joe to take good care of her Lester. And then she turned around and took the next bus back to Waukesha by herself.

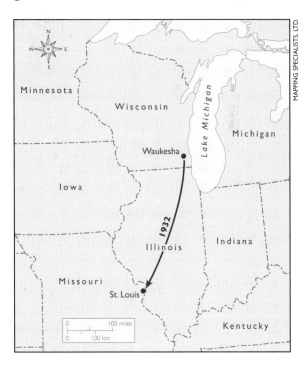

Moving to Saint Louis

forming: putting together   **graduating (graj** oo ay ting): finishing school and receiving a diploma

5

"Rhubarb Red" in Chicago

Joe took Les from the Saint Louis bus station to the
rooming house that would be his new home. There he met
the other members of the radio band, which was called the
Scalawags. Les was still imitating his old hero Pie Plant Pete,
playing in an old-time country **style**. That was a good thing,
because it was exactly what the people at KMOX radio
wanted him to sound like. But the one thing they didn't like
about Les was his nickname. They liked the "Red" part well
enough—after all, it was the color of his hair—but they didn't
think Red Hot Red had the right ring to it. It was Joe who
suggested "**Rhubarb** Red."

The Scalawags' radio show was popular right away, and the
band quickly got hired to play shows all over Saint Louis. Les
was making very good money at this job, $45 a week. That
was enough to allow him to buy his first **professional-grade**

rooming house: a private house in which rooms are rented to different people   scalawags (**skal** i wagz): people
who behave badly while being funny   style: the way in which something is played   rhubarb (**roo** bahrb): a tall
plant with reddish or greenish stems   professional-grade: high-quality

guitar. It was a model called the L-50, made by a company called **Gibson**, one of the most famous guitar makers in America.

Meanwhile, Joe took Les **under his wing**

Les's first job as a **full-time** musician came when he joined the Scalawags and moved to Saint Louis.

and taught him how be a professional musician. Even though Les was a very good guitar player, he had mostly taught himself to play. That meant he had picked up some bad habits that would make it harder to keep improving. Joe helped him to break those habits.

Even though the Scalawags were a hit on the radio, the country was in the middle of the **Great Depression**. Many people were struggling to keep their jobs and put food on

Gibson: gib suhn   **full-time**: all of the time   **under his wing**: guided or protected by someone
Great Depression: a time in the 1930s when many people lost their jobs and businesses closed

One of Les's favorite guitars was his Gibson L-5, which he bought from the Gibson company in Kalamazoo, Michigan, while he and Joe were on the way to Springfield.

their tables. Radio stations were having trouble making enough money to stay in business. Eventually, the Scalawags lost their job at KMOX.

Les was about to pack up and go back home to Waukesha. But just before he was to leave, Joe found the 2 of them a new radio job in Springfield, Missouri. Springfield is about 200 miles south of Saint Louis. There, Joe and Les became a 2-man **act** known as the **Ozark** Apple Knockers. In addition to playing music, they also told **corny** jokes **on the air**.

act: group that performs together   **Ozark**: **oh** zahrk   **corny**: silly and old-fashioned   **on the air**: on the radio

Things went well in Springfield. Les and Joe's act was popular. Les's guitar playing was improving so fast that he caught up with Joe, and even got a little better

The Ozark Apple Knockers: Sunny Joe and Rhubarb Red

than his friend. Then, after several months in Springfield, the pair got a much better job offer. They were hired as radio musicians on WBBM, one of the biggest stations in Chicago.

In 1933, Chicago was the second largest city in the United States. Only New York City was bigger. The Ozark Apple Knockers turned out

Sunny Joe and Les Paul

to be a hit in Chicago, too. Soon Les and Joe were making

29

hundreds of dollars a week! And this was during the worst part of the Great Depression, when millions of Americans were making no money at all.

Up until now, Les and Joe had made a great team. But as Les became more of an adult, he no longer wanted to **go along with** all of Joe's plans. Joe was happy to keep playing old-fashioned country music. But Les had other ideas.

Les could play harmonica and guitar at the same time with the harmonica holder he invented.

go along with: follow

For one thing, Les was fascinated by jazz music. Jazz was started by African Americans musicians. In jazz music, players have a lot of freedom to make up their own melodies and rhythms as they go along. In Chicago, some of the best jazz in the world was being created by jazz musicians like Coleman Hawkins, Roy Eldridge, and Earl Hines. Les wanted to learn how to play like them. One day, Joe announced that they should go to Australia. But Les wanted to stay in Chicago and become a jazz musician. So after 2 years of living and working together, the team split up. But they stayed good friends for the rest of their lives.

Once Les was on his own, he made some big changes. He didn't want to play the old country songs anymore. He wanted to play jazz. And he wanted to play it on piano instead of guitar. And he made another big change. Instead of going by Rhubarb Red, he wanted to be called Les Paul. "Paul" was similar to his real last name, Polsfuss.

Les put together a jazz **trio** and started looking for work. His first professional job as a jazz musician was with his trio,

trio (**tree** oh): a band with 3 members

31

playing as the **backup band** for **comedians**, including Jackie **Gleason** and Joe E. Lewis. Les found other jazz jobs as well, but he soon learned that it was much harder to make a living playing jazz piano than it was playing country music.

Fortunately, Les had made a lot of friends during his days with Joe. One of those friends got him an **audition** for a show on a big Chicago radio station that played a lot of old-time country music. When Les arrived at the station, he saw a familiar face. One of the other musicians waiting to try for the job was

Les takes the stage at Riverside Park in Chicago.

none other than his old hero, Pie Plant Pete! Les almost felt bad for Pete when he beat him out of the job. Now playing as a **solo act**, Les was once again Rhubarb Red, country guitarist

backup band: a band that plays music behind a performer   **comedian**: a professional joke-teller
Gleason: glee suhn   **audition** (aw di shuhn): a test a musician or actor takes to get a place in a band or a part in a play   **solo act**: a performance by one person

32

and harmonica player. But at night, he would find places to be Les Paul, the jazzman.

After a while, Les realized that he would never be a great jazz piano player, so he switched back to guitar. Soon after the switch, Les heard an amazing guitar player who got him excited about the guitar—and jazz— once again. The guitarist's name was **Django Reinhardt**. Django was a **Gypsy** from **Belgium**, a country in Europe. He played jazz faster and better than any guitarist had before.

Les Paul performing as Rhubarb Red on a major Chicago radio station

Django Reinhardt: jang goh **rın** hahrt   **Gypsy** (**jip** see): a term sometimes used for one of the Romany people, who often travel around instead of living in one place   **Belgium: bel** juhm

33

Almost every night, Les would find a jazz club where he could **sit in** with whatever band was playing. Chicago was one of the best cities in the world for jazz, and Les had the chance to play with some of the greatest jazz musicians of the time.

Inspired by Django Reinhardt, Les formed a new band called Les Paul and the **Melody** Kings. The Melody Kings got a

job playing jazz on WIND, one of Chicago's biggest radio stations. Their musical style was similar to Django's.

Les was probably the busiest musician in the world now! At 5:00 in the morning, he was country musician Rhubarb Red. In the afternoon he would **rehearse** with his trio, then play on the radio with the Melody Kings. And

Les was inspired by Gypsy jazz guitarist Django Reinhardt. The 2 were friends for many years.

sit in: join temporarily   **melody**: an arrangement of musical notes that makes a tune   **rehearse**: practice for a public performance

at night he played shows at the jazz clubs. He barely slept at all!

But he was still frustrated with the sound of the guitar. It was hard to make the guitar heard over the louder instruments like drums and trumpets. He knew that the solution to the problem was to build on his old experiments using electricity to **amplify** the sound of the guitar.

Les asked a company called the National String Instrument Company to make him a special guitar with a solid body made out of a single piece of wood. Les also made his own **pickup** for the guitar. The pickup "picks up" the **vibrations** made by the guitar's strings and turns them into an electrical signal. Soon, Les was working on the invention that would make him famous: the solid-body electric guitar.

amplify: make louder   **pickup**: a device that picks up the vibrations from a stringed instrument and changes them into an electrical signal   **vibration**: rapid movement back and forth

How Does an Electric Guitar Work?

When you pluck a guitar string, the string starts to vibrate. Those vibrations are what make the sound, whether it is an acoustic or an electric guitar. Acoustic guitars make the sound louder by having it bounce around inside the hollow part of the guitar. The solid-body electric guitar, the kind Les Paul invented, doesn't have a hollow part. It uses electricity to amplify the sound. An electric guitar has something called a pickup—sometimes 2 or 3 of them—attached to it under the strings. A pickup is made of a magnet wrapped in many coils of thin wire. The pickup takes the string's vibrations and **converts** them into electricity. The electricity travels through the guitar's wiring to a jack, where you

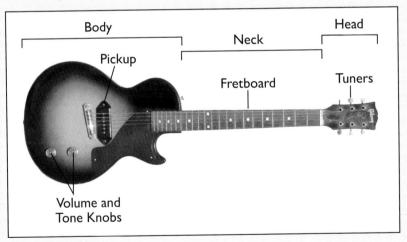

Body Neck Head

Pickup

Fretboard Tuners

Volume and Tone Knobs

The parts of an electric guitar

converts: changes

plug in a guitar cable. The cable carries the electrical signal to an **amplifier**. The amplifier has a speaker in it. The speaker turns the electrical signal back into vibrations, but it makes much bigger vibrations than you originally made by plucking the string. The speaker vibrations make the sound waves that travel to your ears.

Les wasn't quite happy with his first electric guitar, but it was a big step in the right direction. One of the biggest problems was that the solid-body guitar was very heavy. Acoustic guitars are hollow and light. The guitars Les was experimenting with were made out of solid wood, so they weighed a lot more. He did a lot of his experimenting on his old Gibson L-50. It looked terrible because of all the cutting and gluing he had done, but it was his favorite guitar for a long time. Gibson kept sending him their beautiful new models to try out for free, but Les stuck with his beat-up old L-50 for many years.

amplifier: an electronic device used to make the sound of an instrument louder

Les also took the speaker box from a **portable** movie projector and turned it into a guitar amplifier. The amplifier took the electric signal from the pickup and made it louder—much, much louder! This was the first amplifier Les invented that wasn't made out of radio parts. He called it the "Toaster." Later, the Gibson guitar company copied the Toaster. Those copies became some of the earliest guitar amplifiers to be sold to the public.

Les made his first **professional recording** in 1936. This recording would be sold in stores around the country. Performing as Rhubarb Red, Les recorded 4 songs for the Montgomery Ward **record label**. But Les was still more interested in jazz. He

The L-5 Toaster was an early Les Paul amplifier.

portable: able to be carried or moved easily   **professional recording**: a disk or record that is sold
record label: a company that records and sells music

38

was ready to stop performing as Rhubarb Red. The Melody Kings had already broken up, and Les had formed a new group, the Les Paul Trio, with Jimmy Atkins and Ernie Newton. The trio practiced very hard, and soon they felt ready to try to make it in the biggest jazz town in the world: New York City.

6

To the Big Apple and Back

The Les Paul Trio was ready to head for New York. But there was just one problem. Les had **misled** his bandmates to get them to agree to make the move. Les told Jimmy Atkins and Ernie Newton that he had lots of friends in New York, so it would be easy for them to find work. He told them that he was friends with Paul Whiteman, the bandleader of one of the most famous jazz **big bands** in the world. Whiteman had his own show on the NBC radio station in New York.

But Les was not friends with Paul Whiteman. He had never met him. In fact, Les didn't know anybody at all in

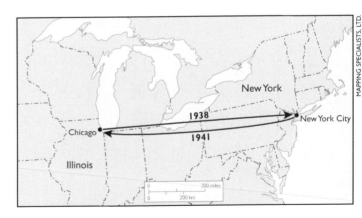

To the Big Apple and back

misled: lied to   **big band**: a large group of musicians in which people play together and by themselves at different points in a song

New York! But Les was sure the trio would succeed in the Big Apple, and he was willing to do anything to get Jimmy and Ernie to move there with him.

Manhattan was a busy, bustling section of New York.

In June 1938, the 3 men packed up Les's car with their clothes and instruments and **hit the road**. In New York, they rented a cheap room near Times Square, a busy area in the middle of Manhattan, the island that makes up the busiest part of New York. Days passed, and Jimmy and Ernie started to wonder when Les was going to see his "great friend" Paul Whiteman about finding them a job.

Manhattan: man **hat** uhn   **hit the road:** started on a trip

Why Is New York Called the "Big Apple"?

Nobody is sure how New York City came to be called the "Big Apple." But the most likely explanation has to do with a man named John Fitzgerald. In the 1920s, Mr. Fitzgerald was a reporter for a newspaper called the *New York Morning Telegraph*. He wrote a regular **column** about horse racing called "Around the Big Apple." Mr. Fitzgerald said that he had first heard the name from stable workers in New Orleans. They called the racetracks in New York the Big Apple because the prize money there was very good. The nickname caught on, especially among jazz musicians in the 1930s and 1940s. Soon all kinds of people used it. Many years later, in 1971, New York City began to use the Big Apple as an official **slogan** for advertising all the great things the city had to offer.

Finally Les could not put it off any longer. He called Paul Whiteman's office on the telephone. He tried to sound like he was Paul's friend, but Mr. Whiteman's secretary could tell Les was **bluffing**. She told him, "Sorry, we're not looking for anybody." Instead of telling his bandmates the truth, Les told them they were to come right over to Whiteman's office. So the trio walked with their instruments 3 blocks to the

column (**kah** luhm): an article by the same writer that appears regularly in a newspaper   **slogan**: a phrase or motto   **bluffing**: lying by pretending to be very confident

building where Whiteman's office was located. When Les saw Mr. Whiteman, he waved and shouted "Hey, Paul!" Of course Mr. Whiteman ignored him and slammed the door. Les didn't know what to do. His friends had just figured out that he had lied to get them to come to New York.

But then something very lucky happened. Another famous bandleader, Fred **Waring**, stepped into the hall. As Mr. Waring waited for the

Paul Whiteman watches a band rehearse at the recording studio.

elevator, Les plugged in his amplifier. The trio started playing one of their best songs. They had to race to finish it before the elevator came. At first Fred did not pay much attention. But he quickly realized that these 3 crazy guys playing in the middle of the hallway were actually very, very good. He

Waring: wer ing

invited them to **cram** into the elevator with him. By the time they got off, the trio had been hired to play on a **nationally broadcast** radio show with Fred Waring and his jazz band, the **Pennsylvanians**.

Les, left, with singer Jimmy Atkins and **bass** player Ernie Newton on Fred Waring's radio show.

---

cram: squeeze together   **nationally broadcast:** played on radio stations across the country
Pennsylvanians: pen suhl **vay** nyuhnz   **bass** (bayss): a tall stringed instrument that plays very low notes

Les went back to Chicago to get his girlfriend, Virginia Webb. On their way back out of the city, they stopped at the **Justice of the Peace**'s office to get married! Then they headed back to New York to start their new life.

Les, Jimmy, and Ernie became **regulars** on Fred Waring's weekly half-hour radio show. They played in his orchestra and also did a song as a trio every week. When Les played with the Pennsylvanians, he would switch back and forth between a regular acoustic guitar and the cheap Gibson electric guitar he had invented. Some of his bandmates didn't want him to use the electric guitar because they were not used to the sound. But Les knew that the electric guitar really helped his solos to be heard over the other instruments. Fred Waring agreed. Soon Les was playing the electric guitar full time.

But Les was still not **satisfied** with the sound of the electric guitar. He still had problems with feedback, which is an unpleasant squealing sound that amplified instruments sometimes make. He knew he could make a better electric guitar with a purer sound.

Justice of the Peace: someone who hears court cases and performs marriages   **regular**: someone who does something often   **satisfied**: happy, content

Les enjoyed his job with Fred Waring. But what he really loved was playing jazz for fun. In New York, he had the chance to play with some of the greatest jazz musicians in the world. He and his friends would often go to **after-hours jam sessions** at little bars in the parts of New York where the best jazz was being made. There they would play with jazz giants like pianist Art Tatum, trumpet player Roy Eldridge, and saxophone players Coleman Hawkins and Lester Young. Les and the trio made their first recordings as a band in 1939. They recorded 4 songs for the Columbia record label, including the famous song "**Swanee** River."

In 1941, Les had a major breakthrough in his work to invent a better electric guitar. Working with a guitar company called **Epiphone**, Les **developed** a guitar he called the "Log." Why did he call it the Log? Well, the Log was basically a thick piece of pine wood 4 inches long and 4 inches wide. It had electrical pickups and a **fretboard** attached. Later, Les added other parts to make it look more like an ordinary guitar. But they were

after-hours: late at night after a business has closed to the public   **jam session**: an informal gathering during which musicians play for fun instead of for an audience   **Swanee**: swah nee   **Epiphone**: ep uh fohn **developed**: made into something better   **fretboard**: the part of a guitar where the player presses down on the strings to make different notes and chords

just **for show**. The Log worked better than any other electric guitar Les had played before.

Things were going very well for Les. But later that year, he had a terrible accident. One day, as he tried to **adjust** some of his electrical equipment, Les received a very strong **electric shock**. He nearly died! Ernie saved his life by quickly turning off the power in the room. Les's hands were badly burned, and the

An older Les poses with his early invention, the Log.

electricity had torn several muscles in his upper body. It took many months for him to **recover**.

---

for show: for decoration   adjust (uh **juhst**): change something slightly   **electric shock**: a sudden, violent jolt of electricity   **recover**: get better

For the first few weeks, he had no feeling in his hands. He was not sure he would ever be able to play the guitar again. But in time, the feeling came back. His wounds began to heal. And perhaps most important, Les gained a new respect for electricity. He would never be that careless again.

While Les was recovering from the electric shock, he decided that he'd accomplished as much as he could on the Fred Waring show. It was time to move on to something new. He wanted to move to California to work with singer Bing Crosby, who was quickly becoming a big star. But the move meant the end of the Les Paul Trio.

Les, Virginia, and their baby son, Rusty, were all packed up and ready to drive across the country when Les got a phone call from an old friend in Chicago. The friend offered Les a job as musical **director** at 2 major Chicago radio stations. The job was easy and would pay more than he had been making with Fred Waring. Les was still recovering from his accident. It seemed like a good idea to take the job in Chicago. Les and

director: the person in charge

his family moved west, but not nearly as far west as they had planned.

Les's new job in Chicago was to hire musicians and plan the music **programming** for the radio stations WJJD and WIND. The work did not require him to do too much, so Les had time for his hands to heal completely. But he still had California on his mind. He knew that as soon as his guitar-playing ability returned, he was going to move to the West Coast.

programming: the set of broadcasts or performances

7

Hollywood Bound

Les still couldn't play much guitar, so he had a lot of time to work on his inventions. In 1941 he took his solid-body

Les with one of his klunkers

guitar, the Log, to the people at the Gibson guitar company to see if they would **manufacture** it. The Gibson people were not impressed. In fact, they thought the Log looked ridiculous! They wanted nothing to do with it. Les was disappointed, but he didn't let it stop him from working to **perfect** his

manufacture (man yoo **fak** chur): make in order to sell   **perfect** (pur **fekt**): make something as good as possible

guitar. He started working on a series of guitars he called "**klunkers**." One of the guitars, made by Epiphone, had a **trap door** on the back, which made it easier for Les to work on the electronic parts inside.

With the klunkers, Les was able to experiment with improving the sound of electric guitars.

By 1943, Les's hands were better. He was able to play the guitar well again, and he sat in with many of the top musicians who passed through Chicago and played at one of his radio stations. But his goal of moving to California and working with Bing Crosby had not changed. So he thanked the people who had hired him at the radio station, packed up his car once again, and moved to Los Angeles, California. Virginia and little Rusty stayed behind in Chicago while Les settled in.

klunker (usually spelled "clunker"): an old, broken-down object or machine   **trap door**: a hidden opening

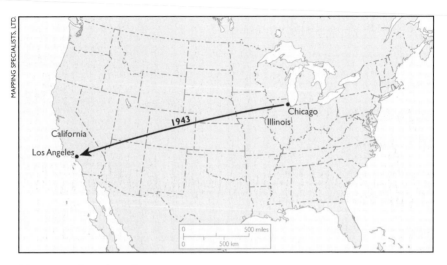

Moving to Los Angeles

It was not difficult for Les to find work in Los Angeles. Many musicians he had met in Chicago were now living there. Soon after arriving, Les put together a new trio, consisting of himself, pianist Joe Rann, and bass player Bob Meyer. The trio began playing at **nightclubs** all over town. But Les had bigger goals. He still wanted to play with Bing Crosby. Remembering how he had **landed** his job with Fred Waring in New York, Les decided to try something similar.

One day, Les and his trio snuck into NBC radio studios when most of the staff were on break and set up their

nightclub: a place where people perform for audiences at night   **landed**: gained or gotten

equipment. When the music director came to ask who they were and what they were doing there, they started to play. The music director was impressed and

Les landed a great job at NBC studios in Los Angeles.

went to find one of the bosses. The boss turned out to be Sid **Strotz**, an old friend of Les's from Chicago. Sid was now a vice-president at NBC and was happy to hire the trio. And just like that, Les and his bandmates became **staff musicians** at NBC.

Les Paul and His Trio started playing whenever they were needed to fill **air time**. Word quickly got around the studio that they were good. Singers who were scheduled to go on the air would often hire them as their backup band. Before long, Les had a lot of new fans in California.

Strotz: strahts   **staff musician**: a musician at a radio or television station who plays whatever music the station needs   **air time**: time during a broadcast

Les and his trio worked at NBC as staff musicians.

Being in Los Angeles brought other opportunities as well. The section of the city known as Hollywood is the center of the American movie business. Before long, Les started appearing on the "**silver screen**." His first movie appearance, along with the trio, was playing a song in a film called *Sensations of 1945*. Soon after that, Les got a tiny part in another movie as a guitar-playing milkman.

It was the middle of World War II. Many of the nation's young men were being called on to serve in the **armed forces**. Les was no exception. He was **drafted** into the army in 1943. Fortunately for Les, the army had a lot of bands. So his military

silver screen: movies   **armed forces**: the military   **drafted**: called up to serve in the armed forces

job would be to play music instead of going into battle. Les was even luckier than that. He became a member of the Armed Forces Radio Service. He was officially stationed on the very same street he already lived on and even continued to live in his own home!

Les was very busy as a military musician. Part of his job was to **produce** programs to entertain the troops for the Armed Forces radio network. He also played as a backup musician for famous singers like Kate Smith and Dinah Shore when they entertained the troops. And he also played guitar with bandleader Meredith Willson's orchestra.

Les was **discharged** from the military in 1944, and he went back to his job at NBC. Because of

An early Les Paul trio. The members of the trio often changed.

produce: create **discharged**: released from military service

the war, the musicians in his band kept switching. But it was always called the Les Paul Trio or Les Paul and His Trio. The group became well-known for being able to play almost any kind of music. They began appearing on many of the biggest radio programs of the time. But the most popular show of all was singer Bing Crosby's. And Les had not yet managed to get Bing's attention. They hadn't even met!

Once again, Les had a plan to "accidentally" land the job he was after. He knew that Bing liked to go alone into a tiny studio at NBC to gather his thoughts before his show. So Les had the trio start practicing

Les had long wanted to work with singer Bing Crosby.

in that very studio when he knew Bing was likely to show up. Sure enough, Bing came in and heard Les play. Just as it had happened twice before, Les's trick worked perfectly. Bing immediately hired Les and his trio to be part of the band on his famous radio show, *Kraft Music Hall*. In 1945, Les and Bing recorded a song called "It's Been a Long, Long Time." The song became a huge hit. Millions of people became familiar with Les's **unique** guitar sound and style because of that recording.

Bing and Les's hit song

As Les did more and more work on the radio and in **recording studios**, he began to realize that he knew more about sound than most of the **sound engineers**. The engineers didn't always know the best place to put the microphones. And they didn't usually have as good an ear as Les for adjusting the recording equipment. They simply had not spent as much time

unique (yoo **neek**): the only one of its kind **recording studio**: a place where performers use special equipment to make records **sound engineer**: someone who controls the sound on a musical recording

thinking about and experimenting with the tools of radio and recording as Les had.

Les got the idea to set up his own recording studio. He began collecting equipment to set up a studio in the garage of his house. What he couldn't find or buy, he built himself. Les's garage studio became a popular hangout for serious sound engineers. And many picky musicians came to him to make their records. They knew that Les could give them the sound they were looking for better than the big record companies.

Les set up his own recording studio in his garage.

8

Les Paul and Mary Ford

One day, the NBC program director came to Les and told him he needed to fill 9 more radio time slots. Les immediately thought of the country act he used to do back in Saint Louis and Chicago as Rhubarb Red. He told the station manager that he could easily throw together a new version of the Rhubarb Red show. All he needed to make it great was a talented female singer. **Gene Autry**, a famous cowboy singer Les had worked with, suggested a woman named Colleen Summers. Les called Colleen the next day and invited her to try out for the part.

It turned out that Colleen was already a big fan of Les Paul, so she was happy to audition for a job with him. Les hired her, and quickly gave her a more "country" sounding name:

Gene Autry: jeen **aw** tree

Mary Lou. The new act went on the air as Rhubarb Red and the Ozark Apple Knockers, **featuring** Mary Lou. Les called Colleen "Mary" from then on.

Mary Ford

By this time, Les and Virginia had separated. They would eventually be **divorced**. Les and Mary began spending almost all of their time together. Soon, they fell deeply in love.

Meanwhile, Les's musical career was soaring. He had a regular **gig** at a popular nightclub called Club Rounders where many Hollywood stars liked to hang out. He played guitar on a hit record by the popular singing group the Andrews Sisters. And in 1946, Les and his trio went on a big tour across the nation as the **opening act** for the Andrews Sisters.

featuring (fee chur ing): including a special participant a musician, usually for a certain number of performances before a more famous person or group   **divorced**: no longer married by law   **gig**: a job for **opening act**: first performance, usually appearing

After the tour, Les spent a lot of time in his garage studio focusing on his favorite activity: something he liked to call "chasing sound." He wanted to create a new guitar sound that was all his own, and he wanted to find new and better ways of capturing that sound on recordings. He also invented a new guitar effect called delay, which

Les and Mary working on a song

Les and his trio opened for the Andrews Sisters, another popular act.

Les "chasing sound" in his home studio

makes a note echo after you play it. Eventually, delay would be used by guitarists everywhere.

Les was also working on a new way to record music. Instead of having to get a whole band together, he wondered what it would be like to play all of the parts himself. Les made his first multitrack recordings using 2 **record machines** to create music in layers. He would record one part on the first machine. Then he would play it back while recording another part to go along with it on the second machine. He could then go back to the first machine and record a third part on a new disk. Now he had 3 parts recorded—all played by one musician.

record machine: a device used to "cut" or record a record

He would go back and forth in that way as many times as he needed to record all of the layers he had thought of. Some people call this back-and-forth way of recording "ping-pong" recording.

After he had experimented for a while, Les put all of his new **techniques** together to record a song called "Lover." "Lover" was the first song he recorded that showed off what came to be known as the "New Sound." In 1947, Les took "Lover" to Capitol Records, a recording company that was just getting started. The people at Capitol loved the New Sound. They were

Les records Mary in their home recording studio.

technique (tek **neek**): a way of doing something that requires skill

63

sure "Lover" would be a hit, and they immediately asked Les to sign a **recording contract**.

Everything was going well for Les. But the good times came crashing to a halt in January 1948. Les and Mary decided to drive all the way from California to Waukesha to visit Les's mother. On the way there, Les began to feel sick. After the visit they began the long drive back home to California. Les continued to get sicker. As they drove through the state of Missouri, Les needed to rest, so Mary took the wheel.

A winter storm started as they passed through Missouri into Oklahoma. The roads were icy and wet, and the car slid off the side of a bridge into a **ravine**. Mary suffered only minor injuries, but Les was hurt very badly. He broke many bones and had **internal** injuries. His right elbow was completely crushed. The doctors also discovered that he had **pneumonia**.

The doctors were not sure Les would live. And even if he did live, they thought he might lose his right arm. Doctors had to take a piece of bone from Les's leg and put it where

recording contract: a legal agreement between a record company and a performer   **ravine** (ruh **veen**): a narrow valley with steep sides   **internal**: inside the body   **pneumonia** (noo **moh** nyuh): a serious illness that causes the lungs to become inflamed and filled with a thick fluid that makes breathing hard

his elbow used to be. The doctors told him that even if he was able to keep his arm, he might never be able to bend his elbow again. Les told the surgeon to position his arm so that his hand was at the same height as his belly button. That way, he might still be able to play the guitar once his arm healed.

About a month after the accident, Capitol Records **released** Les's record, *Lover.* As the company predicted, the **title song** was a huge hit. Les was offered a long gig at the top jazz club in Chicago, the Blue Note. He told the people at the Blue Note that as soon as he was able to play again, he would love to do the show. Playing at the Blue Note gave him something to work toward as he began his long recovery.

It would be months before Les could play the guitar normally. But Les was determined, and he was still an inventor. He **rigged** a special stand that could hold the guitar up. Even though almost his entire upper body was in a cast, the stand allowed him to play. He recorded several more songs for Capitol while his arm slowly healed.

released: made available to the public for the first time   **title song**: a song that has the same name as the record it is from   **rigged**: put together in a casual way using whatever you can find

Even with a cast, Les still played guitar after his accident.

Finally, Les's arm was strong enough, and he was eager to go back to work full time. He and Mary had been working on an act as a **duo**, and they were ready to put it on the air. But first, Mary needed a **stage name**. They decided on Mary Ford. Les and Mary started doing a radio show called *Les Paul and Mary Ford at Home*. Until this time, radio shows were done live, not recorded on tape ahead of time. But that was about to change.

In 1949, Les received a gift from his friend Bing Crosby that changed his life and changed the future of recorded music. Bing gave Les the best kind of tape recorder being made at the time, an Ampex 300. The new machine gave Les an amazing idea. He figured out that by adding an extra **head**

duo (**doo** oh): a band with 2 members   **stage name**: a name used by a performer for professional purposes
head: the part of a tape recorder that records music onto the tape

to the Ampex 300, he could record another part on the same tape while he listened to the first part. Les had just invented the first machine capable of multitrack recording! Now, instead of using several recorders, he would be able to use *one* recorder to record many parts into one song. He

Les Paul and Mary Ford

could record one part, then add more layers of music on top of that, slowly building a song that had many instruments and voices.

Les used the Ampex 300 to create the first multitrack recorder.

67

Armed with his new recorder, Les and Mary traveled
to Chicago to work at the Blue Note jazz club, just as they
had promised after Les's accident. After each performance,
they would go back to their hotel room and work on their
radio show, recording it with the multitrack recorder. In
the morning, they would mail the tape of the show back to
California to be played on the radio. This was a very busy,
very happy time for Les and Mary. They spent nearly all their
time working and playing together. On December 29, 1949,
the pair got married in Milwaukee, Wisconsin.

9

More Wonders from the Wizard

Things couldn't have been much better for Les and Mary in 1950. They had just gotten married. Les had just recorded 3 **instrumental** songs that had been big hits. And many clubs and music **venues** asked them to come and play live shows. Les used the money he was earning to pay off the huge medical bills from the accident.

By this time, Les and Mary were living in New York, though they still owned a house in Los Angeles. In 1951 they released a new recording of the song "How High the Moon." This song had been recorded by many different musicians, and it had never been a big hit. But Les and Mary's version was unique. It used Les's new multitrack-recording techniques. "How High the Moon" quickly rose to number one on the **charts** and stayed there for many weeks! Another song of theirs, "Mockingbird Hill," was a big hit at the same

instrumental: a song that has just instruments, but no singing   **venue** (ven **yoo**): the place where a performance is given   **charts**: the list of recorded music that shows which is most popular during a given time

time. Radio stations were playing their songs constantly. Television was still very new, and Les and Mary were invited to be on one of the most popular TV programs, the *Ed Sullivan Show*.

Les wanted to use the multilayered sounds of their recordings at the duo's live performances. It took a lot of time and effort, but with help from local sound engineers, Les made it work. Later, Les built a piece of equipment that did what the engineers had been doing. That piece of equipment became known as the "Les **Paulverizer**." Les had the Paulverizer set up so that he could control it from his guitar while onstage.

"How High the Moon" used multitrack recording and became a hit in 1951.

Paulverizer: pawl ver ɪ zur

Meanwhile, Les continued to think about how to improve the electric guitar. Before he had made his hit recordings, Les spent a lot of time talking about

70

electric guitars with friends, including Leo Fender. Leo had shown Les the electric guitar he was working on, and Les could see that Leo's ideas were almost as good as his own.

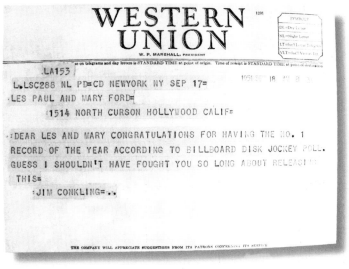

A telegram congratulates Les and Mary on the success of "How High the Moon."

Leo's work would soon lead to a decent electric guitar.

Gibson, the same company that had rejected the Log years earlier, was now eager to work with Les on his design for the electric guitar. The company quickly went to work with Les to develop a solid-body electric guitar. In 1952, Gibson started to manufacture the Gibson

The Paulverizer sits on top of a large amplifier.

71

Les Paul electric guitar. Les began playing Gibson Les Paul guitars at all of his live shows. But he still preferred to use his old klunkers that he had worked on himself when he recorded in the studio.

Because Les had his own portable recording studio, Les and Mary could record songs wherever they happened to be. Instead of having to go to a special studio to record a song like most musicians, they could stay on the road for months at a time. That way, they could continue to perform live shows while still making new records. They recorded hits in hotel rooms, basements, and anywhere they found themselves.

By this time, television was becoming more important, and Les had realized that the radio show

Les helped Gibson develop a solid-body electric guitar.

in California had **run its course**. He also realized that even though he loved his garage studio, he no longer needed it to make good recordings.

Most television stations were in New York, and it made sense for Les and Mary to move back to the East Coast.

Just as they were making the decision to move, they got amazing news. They were offered their very own TV show in New York, the *Les Paul and Mary Ford Show*. The

Les's portable recording studio

TV show **sealed the deal**. Les and Mary moved into a beautiful new house in **Mahwah**, New Jersey, just across from New York City. And they set out to become television stars.

run its course: was no longer useful or important   sealed the deal: made the decision final
Mahwah: **mah** wuh

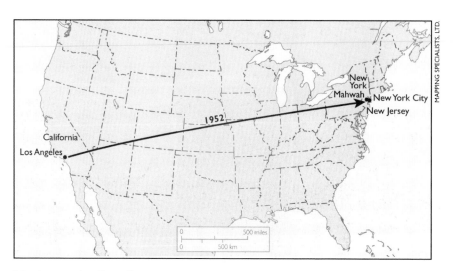

Moving to the East Coast

It didn't take long for Les and Mary to become famous. They had thousands of fans. They played for US presidents. They even became popular in other countries. They went to England and played for Queen Elizabeth! They recorded hit after hit. Their 1953 recording "**Vaya Con Dios**," Spanish for "Go with God," was their biggest hit yet.

That year, while making their television show, Les got another idea for a huge breakthrough in multitrack recording. With his earlier machines, it was not possible to make changes to each separate part. Once a new layer was

Vaya Con Dios: vı ah kohn dee **ohs**

74

recorded, all the parts recorded so far had to be treated like a single part.

It took Les until 1957 to perfect his new machine. But the hard work was worth it. The 8-track recorder allowed a musician to record and **edit**

Les and Mary on the set of their television show

each part **independently**. This breakthrough would change the way musicians everywhere made records.

In the late 1950s, Les and Mary decided to start a family. They adopted a daughter, Colleen, in 1958. The very next year, they had a baby boy, Robert. By this time, rock and roll was **overtaking** jazz as America's most popular music. As a

edit: change or revise to make something better   **independently**: on its own   **overtaking**: catching up and passing by

Les and Mary became very popular in the United States and around the world.

result, Les and Mary's songs were not as successful as they had been just a few years earlier. But it had been a **good run**. Between 1948, when their first hit, "Lover," was released, and 1957, the last year they had a song on the charts, Les and Mary had released 40 **singles** and sold over 10 million records!

good run: a successful series of events **single**: a recording with one song

76

Unfortunately, as their popularity dropped, the strain of so much work was also causing problems in their marriage. Mary wanted them to quit performing

The 8-track recorder

entirely. After all, they already had as much money as they would ever need. And they had a family to raise. But Les loved music and couldn't imagine stopping. Les and Mary were divorced in 1964.

Meanwhile, the electric guitar had fallen on **hard times**. People were getting excited about folk music, a form of music that was mostly played on acoustic instruments. Gibson was planning to get out of the electric instrument business. But Les knew that there was a new generation of young guitarists who loved to play on electric instruments. Many of those young guitarists, such as Jimmy Page (of the rock band Led

hard times: lack of popularity

Zeppelin) and Jeff Beck went on to become the most famous musicians of their time. Les was able to convince the people at Gibson to make a new generation of Les Paul guitars for the new generation of guitar players.

The year after the divorce, Les decided to end his performing career. He'd had enough of the crazy lifestyle of the performing musician. He was tired of the constant travel. And he wanted to spend more time working on his inventions. He worked with the Gibson Company on new designs for the Les Paul **line** of guitars. Les turned out to be right about the popularity of the electric guitar. Young musicians loved the Les Paul guitar, and it became a favorite of rock stars all over the world.

How a Les Paul guitar is made

Zeppelin: zep luhn   **line**: a set of products like clothing or furniture designed by one person or company, but with a range of styles, prices, and quality

10

Les Paul, the Living Legend

It was the early 1970s, and things were not going well for Les. His hearing had been damaged by 2 separate accidents. Although he was able to hear with the help of hearing aids, this was still a terrible blow to somebody whose hearing was so important to his favorite activities. He was also suffering from **arthritis**, a disease that made it hard to bend his fingers. The arthritis made it impossible for Les to play the guitar the way he used to. As a result, he was hardly playing the guitar at all.

Then one day in 1972, a friend asked Les to **fill in** for another guitarist at a small nightclub. Les was not sure he was ready for the job, but he said yes anyway. Soon, people heard that Les was playing. Many famous people showed up to watch and listen. The show was a success, and it made Les feel better about playing in public again. He started performing

arthritis (ahr **thri** tis): a disease that causes joints to become swollen and painful   **fill in**: join in place of someone else temporarily

regularly again, though not nearly as much as he had in the past. In 1975, he played a big show at New York's famous **Carnegie** Hall.

Around the same time, Les got a phone call from Chet Atkins. Chet was the younger brother of Les's old bandmate Jimmy Atkins, from the Les Paul Trio on Fred Waring's show. Chet himself was a **legendary** guitarist. Chet suggested that the 2 of them record an album together. They did just that, and the album, *Chester and Lester*, was a huge success. Many fans—old and new—became interested in Les's amazing musical career. The praise didn't stop there. In 1976, *Chester and Lester* won a Grammy Award, the highest honor in the American music industry.

A few years later, Les ran into more health problems. Several **blood vessels** near his heart were clogged. The doctors said Les wouldn't survive surgery. They refused to do the operation. But Les's mother **persuaded** Les to find another doctor who was willing to operate. After the surgery, it took Les a long time to get his strength back. Having been close

---

Carnegie: kahr nuh gee   **legendary**: very famous for a long time   **blood vessel**: a tube in the body through which blood flows   **persuaded** (per **sway** ded): convinced

to death, Les thought hard about how he wanted to live the rest of his life. He realized that playing music was still the thing that made him happiest.

Chester and Lester, 1976

In 1984, Les started to play a regular weekly show at a New York club called Fat Tuesday's. A lot of his old musician friends started showing up to play along with Les. Young rock musicians came to Fat Tuesday's to meet their hero, Les Paul. Even though he had never been as famous as other stars, Les was put into the Rock and Roll Hall of Fame in 1988. Rock and roll as we know it would not exist without Les' inventions.

In the mid-1990s, Fat Tuesday's closed. Les moved his regular gig to a different club in New York, the **Iridium** Jazz Club. By this time, Les's arthritis had gotten much worse. He could hardly bend his fingers at all. But he had learned something over the years: you don't have to play fast in order to make great music. Sometimes playing just one note in just the right way at just the right time is better than showing off with a **flurry** of notes.

Les played guitar every week for over 12 years at the Iridium Jazz Club in New York.

Les's playing style had changed, but he was still a great musician, especially inside, where it counts the most. That spirit kept him strong. Les was still playing at Iridium 12 years later, when he was over 90 years old!

Even though it had been a long time since Les lived in Wisconsin, he always

Iridium: i **rid** ee uhm   **flurry**: a fast burst

considered Waukesha to be his hometown. He was introduced everywhere as "Les Paul, the Wizard of Waukesha." Museums all over the world have tried to get Les to give them some of his early inventions,

Les at the Iridium

such as the guitars he experimented on and the recorders and amplifiers he built. But Les was **loyal** to Waukesha.

In 2007, Les returned home to Waukesha to play a special benefit concert to raise money for a permanent exhibit at the Waukesha County Historical Society and Museum. That same year, the Public Broadcasting Service (PBS) showed a **documentary** called *Les Paul: Chasing Sound*. And in June 2008, Discovery World, a science and technology museum in Milwaukee, opened an exhibit about Les Paul. *Les Paul's House of Sound* is an exhibit that traces Les's path from his boyhood in Waukesha through his inventions and recordings

loyal: firm in supporting someone or something   **documentary**: a movie or television program about real people and events

83

all the way into his 90s. Les came to Wisconsin again to play a special concert celebrating the grand opening of the Discovery World exhibit.

Les was still going strong at age 93 when the Discovery World exhibit opened. Like anybody that age, he was always dealing with physical problems. But these problems didn't stop him from playing his regular show at Iridium. And they didn't stop him from thinking about inventions. Sometimes a person's own challenges can inspire them to have great ideas. Even in his 90s, Les used his knowledge of amplifiers to come up with a new and better type of hearing aid.

Les Paul's House of Sound exhibit at Discovery World in Milwaukee

That's exactly what Les tried to do for his entire life: make a perfect sound and create a perfect way for people to hear it.

But nobody can live forever. Les died from pneumonia in 2009 at the age of 94. Even though his death was sad, musicians and music lovers all over the world celebrated the life of one of most important people in the history of music. Les chose to be buried in his beloved Waukesha next to his mother.

Les lives on in the recordings he made of his own music. And he lives on in all of the other music that could only be made or heard because of Les's many inventions.

Checking out the exhibit

Les was still going strong in his 90s.

Appendix

Les's Time Line

1915 — Lester William Polsfuss is born in Waukesha, Wisconsin, on June 9.

1927 — Les gets his first guitar from the Sears & Roebuck catalog.

1932 — Les drops out of high school to join Sunny Joe Wolverton in Saint Louis.

1934 — Les changes his stage name from Rhubarb Red to Les Paul.

1938 — Les moves to New York City and joins Fred Waring and the Pennsylvanians on NBC radio.

1941 — Les invents the "Log," his first solid-body electric guitar. Later that year he is badly injured when he receives an electric shock in his studio.

1943 — Les moves to Los Angeles to pursue his dream of working with Bing Crosby.

1945 — Les meets Colleen Summers (who is later known as Mary Ford).

1947 — Les introduces multitracking to the world with the release of "Lover."

1948 — Les is badly injured when his car skids off a bridge in a snowstorm on US Route 66.

1949 — Les marries singer Mary Ford.

1950 — *The Les Paul Show*, featuring Les and Mary, debuts on NBC Radio.

1951 — "How High the Moon" becomes a number one hit.

1952 — Gibson Guitar Company introduces the Les Paul gold-top solid-body electric guitar.

Les and Mary move to New Jersey and start making the TV series *Les Paul and Mary Ford at Home*, which debuts in October 1953.

1953 — "Vaya Con Dios" becomes a number one hit.

Ampex produces the first 8-track tape recorder, based on Les's design.

1964 — Les and Mary divorce.

1965 — Les retires from performing.

1972 — Les comes out of retirement when he fills in for a friend at a New York night club.

1975 — Les performs at Carnegie Hall.

1976 — Les and Chet Atkins release the album *Chester and Lester*, which wins a Grammy Award for Best Country Instrumental Performance.

1980 — Les has heart bypass surgery.

1983 — Les receives the Grammy Lifetime Achievement Award.

1984 — Les begins a regular Monday night gig at Fat Tuesday's.

1988 — Les is inducted into the Rock and Roll Hall of Fame.

1996 — Les begins a regular Monday night gig at Iridium after Fat Tuesday's closes.

2001 — Les receives a Technical Grammy.

2005 — Les is inducted into the National Inventors Hall of Fame, the Songwriters Hall of Fame, and the Grammy Hall of Fame.

Les records *Les Paul & Friends*, his first album in 30 years. He receives Grammy awards for 2 of its songs—Best Pop Instrumental Performance for "Caravan" and Best Rock Instrumental for "69 Freedom Special."

2007 — Les receives the National Medal of Arts from President George W. Bush.

2008 — *Les Paul's House of Sound* exhibit opens at Discovery World in Milwaukee.

2009 — Les dies on August 12. He is buried in Waukesha's Prairie Home Cemetery next to his mother.

Selected Discography

Singles

"It's Been a Long, Long Time"—Bing Crosby & Les Paul (1945)

"Rumors Are Flying"—Andrews Sisters & Les Paul (1946)

"Lover (When You're Near Me)" (1948)

"Brazil" (1948)

"What is this Thing Called Love?" (1948)

"Nola" (1950)

"Goofus" (1950)

"Little Rock 69 Getaway" (1950/1951)

"Tennessee Waltz" —Les Paul & Mary Ford (1950/1951)

"Mockingbird Hill" —Les Paul & Mary Ford (1951)

"How High the Moon" —Les Paul & Mary Ford (1951)

"I Wish I Had Never Seen Sunshine" —Les Paul & Mary Ford (1951)

"The World Is Waiting for the Sunrise" —Les Paul & Mary Ford (1951)

"Just One More Chance" —Les Paul & Mary Ford (1951)

"Jazz Me Blues" (1951)

"Josephine" (1951)

"Whispering" (1951)

"Jingle Bells" (1951/1952)

"Tiger Rag" —Les Paul & Mary Ford (1952)

"I'm Confessin' (That I Love You)" —Les Paul & Mary Ford (1952)

"Carioca" (1952)

"In the Good Old Summertime" —Les Paul & Mary Ford (1952)

"Smoke Rings" —Les Paul & Mary Ford (1952)

"Meet Mister Callaghan" (1952)

"Take Me in Your Arms and Hold Me" —Les Paul & Mary Ford (1952)

"Lady of Spain" (1952)

"My Baby's Coming Home" —Les Paul & Mary Ford (1952)

"Bye Bye Blues" —Les Paul & Mary Ford (1953)

"I'm Sitting on Top of the World" —Les Paul & Mary Ford (1953)

"Sleep" (Fred Waring's theme song) (1953)

"Vaya Con Dios" —Les Paul & Mary Ford (1953)

"Johnny (Is the Boy for Me)" —Les Paul & Mary Ford (1953)

"Don'cha Hear Them Bells" —Les Paul & Mary Ford (1953)

"The Kangaroo" (1953)

"I Really Don't Want to Know" —Les Paul & Mary Ford (1954)

"I'm a Fool to Care" —Les Paul & Mary Ford (1954)

"Whither Thou Goest" —Les Paul & Mary Ford (1954)

"Mandolino" —Les Paul & Mary Ford (1954)

"Song in Blue" —Les Paul & Mary Ford (1954)

"Hummingbird" —Les Paul & Mary Ford (1955)

"Amukiriki (The Lord Willing)" —Les Paul & Mary Ford (1955)

"Magic Melody" —Les Paul & Mary Ford (1955)

"Texas Lady" —Les Paul & Mary Ford (1956)

"Moritat" (theme from "Three Penny Opera") (1956)

"Nuevo Laredo" —Les Paul & Mary Ford (1956)

"Cinco Robles (Five Oaks)" —Les Paul & Mary Ford (1957)

"Put a Ring on my Finger" —Les Paul & Mary Ford (1958)

"Jura (I Swear I Love You)" —Les Paul & Mary Ford (1961)

"Love Sneakin' Up on You" —Les Paul, Joss Stone, & Sting (2005)

Albums

Hawaiian Paradise (1949)

The Hit Makers! (1950)

The New Sound (1950)

Les Paul's New Sound, Volume 2 (1951)

Bye Bye Blues! (1952)

Les and Mary (1955)

Time to Dream (1957)

Lover's Luau (1959)

Bouquet of Roses (1962)

Warm and Wonderful (1962)

Swingin' South (1963)

Fabulous Les Paul and Mary Ford (1965)

Les Paul Now! (1968)

The Guitar Artistry of Les Paul (1971)

Chester and Lester (1976)

Guitar Monsters (1977)

Les Paul: The Legend and the Legacy (1991; re-released in 1996; a 4-CD box set chronicling his years with Capitol Records)

The Best of the Capitol Masters: Selections from "The Legend and the Legacy" Box Set (1992)

California Melodies (2003)

Les Paul & Friends: American Made World Played (2005)

Les Paul & Friends: A Tribute to a Legend (2008)

Glossary

Pronunciation Key

a c<u>a</u>t (kat), pl<u>ai</u>d (plad),
     h<u>a</u>lf (haf)

ah f<u>a</u>ther (**fah** THur),
      h<u>ea</u>rt (hahrt)

air c<u>a</u>rry (**kair** ee), b<u>ear</u> (bair),
       wh<u>ere</u> (whair)

aw <u>a</u>ll (awl), l<u>aw</u> (law),
      b<u>ou</u>ght (bawt)

ay s<u>ay</u> (say), br<u>ea</u>k (brayk),
      v<u>ei</u>n (vayn)

e b<u>e</u>t (bet), s<u>a</u>ys (sez),
     d<u>ea</u>f (def)

ee b<u>ee</u> (bee), t<u>ea</u>m (teem),
      f<u>ea</u>r (feer)

i b<u>i</u>t (bit), w<u>o</u>men (**wim** uhn),
     b<u>ui</u>ld (bild)

ɪ <u>i</u>ce (ɪs), l<u>ie</u> (lɪ), sk<u>y</u> (skɪ)

o h<u>o</u>t (hot), w<u>a</u>tch (wotch)

oh <u>o</u>pen (**oh** puhn), s<u>ew</u> (soh)

oi b<u>oi</u>l (boil), b<u>oy</u> (boi)

oo p<u>oo</u>l (pool), m<u>o</u>ve (moov),
      sh<u>oe</u> (shoo)

or <u>or</u>der (**or** dur), m<u>ore</u> (mor)

ou h<u>ou</u>se (hous), n<u>ow</u> (nou)

u g<u>oo</u>d (gud), sh<u>ou</u>ld (shud)

uh c<u>u</u>p (kuhp), fl<u>oo</u>d (fluhd),
      b<u>utt</u>on (**buht** uhn)

ur b<u>ur</u>n (burn), p<u>ear</u>l (purl),
      b<u>ir</u>d (burd)

yoo <u>u</u>se (yooz), f<u>ew</u> (fyoo),
       v<u>iew</u> (vyoo)

hw <u>wh</u>at (hwuht), <u>wh</u>en (hwen)

TH <u>th</u>at (THat), brea<u>the</u> (breeTH)

zh mea<u>s</u>ure (**mezh** ur),
      gara<u>ge</u> (guh **razh**)

accompanied: played along on a musical instrument

accomplish: do or complete something successfully

acoustic (uh **koo** stik): doesn't use electricity to change the sound or make it louder

act: group that performs together

adjust (uh **juhst**): move or change something slightly

after-hours: late at night after a business has closed to the public

air time: time during a broadcast

amplifier: an electronic device used to make the sound of an instrument louder

amplify: make louder

analog (**an** uh log): showing information with moving parts, instead of numbers

antenna (an **ten** uh): a piece of metal or wire used to send or receive radio signals

appeared: performed on television, radio, or live

approved: had a good opinion

armed forces: the military

arthritis (ahr **thrı** tis): a disease that causes joints to become swollen and painful

audition (aw **di** shuhn): a test a musician or actor takes to get a place in a band or a part in a play

backup band: a band that plays music behind a performer

bass (bayss): a tall stringed instrument that plays very low notes

belt: a circular band of rubber used to transfer motion from one part of a machine to another

big band: a large group of musicians in which people play together and by themselves at different points in a song

blood vessel: a tube in the body through which blood flows

bluffing: lying by pretending to be very confident

bridge: the thin piece of wood or plastic that holds a guitar's strings above the body of the instrument

broadcasting: sending out a radio or television program to an audience

carry: travel over a distance

catalog: a magazine listing things you can buy from a company

charts: the list of recorded music that shows which is most popular during a given time

chord (kord): 2 or more musical notes played at the same time

column (**kah** luhm): an article by the same writer that appears regularly in a newspaper

comedian: a professional joke-teller

conduct: allow something to pass through

converts: changes

corny: silly and old-fashioned

cram: squeeze together

crank up: make something run by turning a crank

developed: made into something better

device: a piece of equipment that does a particular job

devised: thought of a new way to do or create something

director: the person in charge

discharged: released from military service

disk: a flat, circular object

divorced: no longer married by law

documentary: a movie or television program about real people and events

drafted: called up to serve in the armed forces

drive-in: a restaurant where customers are served food in their cars

duo (**doo** oh): a band with 2 members

edit: change or revise to make something better

electric shock: a sudden, violent jolt of electricity

electronics: appliances and equipment, such as microwave ovens, computers, televisions, and radar, that work by means of electricity

engineer: someone who is specially trained to build and maintain machines

entertainer: someone who performs in public

featuring (**fee** chur ing): including a special participant

fill in: join in place of someone else temporarily

flurry: a fast burst

flywheel: a heavy wheel that turns at a steady speed to make a machine run smoothly

for show: for decoration

forming: putting together

fretboard: the part of a guitar where the player presses down on the strings to make different notes and chords

full-time: all of the time

gambling: betting money on the outcome of a race, game, or contest

gig: a job for a musician, usually for a certain number of performances

go along with: follow

good run: a successful series of events

graduating (**graj** oo ay ting): finishing school and receiving a diploma

Great Depression: a time in the 1930s when many people lost their jobs and businesses closed

Gypsy (**jip** see): a term sometimes used for one of the Romany people, who often travel around instead of living in one place

hard times: lack of popularity

harmonica: a small musical instrument that you play by blowing out and breathing in through the mouthpiece

harmony: the sounding of 2 or more musical notes that go well together

head: the part of a tape recorder that records music onto the tape

hillbilly: a type of country music from the South, often played on fiddles, banjos, and guitars

hit: something that becomes popular or successful

hit the road: started on a trip

imitate: copy or mimic

independently: on its own

instrumental: a song that has just instruments, but no singing

internal: inside the body

jam session: an informal gathering during which musicians play for fun instead of for an audience

Justice of the Peace: someone who hears court cases and performs marriages

klunker (usually spelled "clunker"): an old, broken-down object or machine

laboratory (**lab** ruh tor ree): a room that has special equipment for people to use in scientific experiments

landed: gained or gotten

legend: someone who is famous or well-known for something they've done

legendary: very famous for a long time

line: a set of products like clothing or furniture designed by one person or company, but with a range of styles, prices, and quality

live (lɪv): broadcast while actually being performed, not recorded before

loyal: firm in supporting someone or something

manufacture (man yoo **fak** chur): make in order to sell

mechanic (muh **kan** ik): a person who repairs machines

melody: an arrangement of musical notes that makes a tune

misled: lied to

model: a particular type or design of a product

multitrack recording: a recording method in which many different parts are recorded at different times into one song

nationally broadcast: played on radio stations across the country

natural: a person who has a special talent or ability

nightclub: a place where people perform for audiences at night

on the air: on the radio

on tour: traveling to different places to perform

opening act: first performance, usually appearing before a more famous person or group

overtaking: catching up and passing by

passion (**pash** uhn): great interest

perfect (pur **fekt**): make something as good as possible

persuaded (per **sway** ded): convinced

pickup: a device that picks up the vibrations from a stringed instrument and changes them into an electrical signal

phonograph (**foh** nuh graf): an old-fashioned record player that used a crank instead of being plugged in

pitch: the highness or lowness of a musical sound

player piano: a piano that can play by itself by reading holes punched in a roll of paper

pneumonia (noo **moh** nyuh): a serious illness that causes the lungs to become inflamed and filled with a thick fluid that makes breathing hard

portable: able to be carried or moved easily

produce: create

professional: making money doing something that others do for fun

professional recording: a disk or record that is sold

professional-grade: high-quality

programming: the set of broadcasts or performances

radio musician: someone who performs music live on the radio

ravine (ruh **veen**): a narrow valley with steep sides

record label: a company that records and sells music

record machine: a device used to "cut" or record a record

recording contract: a legal agreement between a record company and a performer

recording studio: a place where performers use special equipment to make records

recover: get better

regular: someone who does something often

rehearse: practice for a public performance

released: made available to the public for the first time

rely: depend on

rhubarb (**roo** bahrb): a tall plant with reddish or greenish stems

rigged: put together in a casual way using whatever you can find

rooming house: a private house in which rooms are rented to different people

run its course: was no longer useful or important

satisfied: happy, content

scalawags (**skal** i wagz): people who behave badly while being funny

sealed the deal: made the decision final

separated: stopped living together as husband and wife

series: a set of items that come one after another

silver screen: movies

single: a recording with one song

sit in: join temporarily

slogan: a phrase or motto

solo act: a performance by one person

sound engineer: someone who controls the sound on a musical recording

sound quality: the degree of excellence of the sound

staff musician: a musician at a radio or television station who plays whatever music the station needs

stage name: a name used by a performer for professional purposes

style: the way in which something is played

supportive: helping or encouraging someone

technique (tek **neek**): a way of doing something that requires skill

technological breakthrough: a discovery that solves a problem in the fields of science and engineering

telegraph: a device for sending messages long distances by wire or radio using a code of electrical signals

tip: a helpful piece of advice

tips: money given to someone as thanks for service

title song: a song that has the same name as the record it is from

tone arm: the arm of a phonograph that holds the needle that reads the record

touring: traveling to different places to perform

transmitter: a device for sending out radio waves

trap door: a hidden opening

trial and error: the process of trying or testing something and learning from mistakes

trio (**tree** oh): a band with 3 members

under his wing: guided or protected by someone

unique (yoo **neek**): the only one of its kind

venue (**ven** yoo): the place where a performance is given

vibration: rapid movement back and forth

Reading Group Guide and Activities

Discussion Questions

🐾 Les's mother was very supportive of his musical ambitions. Was she right to let him leave home so early to follow his dreams? Do you think he would have succeeded in the same way if she had not?

🐾 Les was fascinated by music from a young age, and he never strayed from his dream to be a famous musician and inventor. Do you have a passion? What are your hopes and dreams? How do you plan to achieve them?

🐾 At 3 points in the story, Les "lands" a job by playing in front of someone famous. Why do you think he succeeded? What other risks did Les take to succeed? Would you take the same risks? Why or why not?

Activities

🐾 Build a simple crystal radio with your class using instructions from a website such as www.sciencebuddies.com. Have a contest to see who can pick up the most radio stations, who can get the clearest sound, and who can pick up the station that is farthest away.

🐾 Imagine you are Les Paul on the road with Rube Tronson and His Texas Cowboys. Write a week's worth of diary entries about life as a 15-year-old touring musician. What's it like to get up on stage every night? Do you get homesick? What new music are you learning? What did you do during the day?

🐾 Pretend you're a music reviewer. Listen to one of Les's hit songs such as "How High the Moon" or "Vaya Con Dios" and write a review of what you liked, what you didn't, and why. Who would you recommend Les's music to?

🐾 One of the most popular models of electric guitar is named after Les Paul. With your class, visit a music store and take a look at a Les Paul guitar, or if one is available at your school, look at one during music class. Notice what makes it similar to other guitars, and what makes it different. If you are brave enough, and if the store workers or music teacher will allow it, try to play a few notes on it yourself.

To Learn More about Les Paul and the Electric Guitar

Les Paul: Chasing Sound. Directed by John Paulson. American Masters series, Icon Television Music, Inc. and Education Broadcasting Corp. 2007. DVD.

Barber, Nicola. *Music: An A-Z Guide*. New York: F. Watts, 2001.

Chapman, Richard. *The New Complete Guitarist*. London: DK Publishing, 2003.

Claybourne, Anna. *The Science of a Guitar: The Science of Sound*. New York: Gareth Stevens Publishing, 2009.

Isherwood, Millicent. *The Guitar*. Oxford: Oxford University Press, Music Dept., 1984.

Mankato, Rita Storey. *The Violin and Other Stringed Instruments*. Minneapolis: Smart Apple Media, 2010.

Masino, Susan. *Famous Wisconsin Musicians*. Oregon, WI: Badger Books, 2003.

Paul, Les and Michael Cochran. *Les Paul: In His Own Words*. West Plains, MO: Russ Cochran, 2005.

Sabbeth, Alex. *Rubber-Band Banjos and a Java Jive Bass: Projects and Activities on the Science of Music and Sound*. San Francisco: Jossey-Bass, 1997.

Acknowledgments

Even a little book like this one takes a big group effort to put together. First and foremost, I would like to thank Les Paul himself, who took the time to talk to me about his experiences and his ideas about life and music. Les passed away not long after our conversation, and I feel very lucky to have had the opportunity to chat with him while he was not only still alive but still actively making music. I am also very grateful for the help of Sue Baker for her careful review of the manuscript and Michael Braunstein for his invaluable help in making sure we got the story completely right and providing access to many wonderful pictures from Les's archives at the Les Paul Foundation.

I was fortunate to have access to several earlier collections of Les's thoughts and memories. Particularly helpful were the book *Les Paul: In His Own Words,* which Les wrote in collaboration with Michael Cochran, and the PBS biography *Les Paul: Chasing Sound,* part of the *American Masters* series. These sources stood out among the many interviews and articles that were helpful in gathering the information to write this book.

I also owe a huge thank you to Sara Phillips and Bobbie Malone of the Wisconsin Historical Society for their support and much-needed prodding to make sure the project continued to creep through myriad delays and obstacles toward completion.

Music is such an important part of what makes us human, and Les Paul contributed as much as just about anybody in modern history to the way we make and listen to popular music today. I hope that reading about his life, his innovations, and his unique ability to overcome challenges inspires at least a few young people to find joy doing what Les spent his entire life doing: chasing sound.

Index

This index points you to the pages where you can read about persons, places, and ideas. If you do not find the word you are looking for, try to think of another word that means about the same thing.

When you see a page number in **bold** it means there is a picture on that page.